IS A DOLPHIN A FISH?

Questions and Answers About Dolphins

W9-CNB-706

BY MELVIN AND GILDA BERGER
ILLUSTRATED BY KAREN CARR

SCHOLASTIC REFERENCE

CONTENTS

KEY TO ABBREVIATIONS
cm = centimeter/centimetre
kg = kilogram
km = kilometer/kilometre
kph = kilometers/kilometres per hour
m = meter/metre
mm = millimeter/millimetre
°C = degrees Celsius
t = tonnes

Text copyright © 2001 by Melvin and Gilda Berger
Illustrations copyright © 2001 by Karen Carr
All rights reserved. Published by Scholastic Inc.
SCHOLASTIC and associated logos are trademarks and/or registered trademarks of Scholastic Inc.

No part of this publication may be reproduced, or stored in a retrieval system, or transmitted in any form or by any means, electronic, mechanical, photocopying, recording, or otherwise, without written permission of the publisher. For information regarding permission, write to Scholastic Inc., Attention: Permissions Department, 557 Broadway, New York, NY 10012.

Library of Congress Cataloging-in-Publication Data

Berger, Melvin
    Is a dolphin a fish? : questions and answers about dolphins/ by Melvin and Gilda
    Berger ; illustrated by Karen Carr.
        p. cm. — (Scholastic question and answer series)
    1. Dolphin—Miscellanea—Juvenile literature. [1. Dolphins—Miscellanea. 2. Questions
    and answers.] I. Berger, Gilda. II. Carr, Karen, 1960- ill. III. Title.
    QL737.C432 B47 2001   599.53—dc21   2001020459

ISBN 0-439-26667-X

10 9 8 7 6 5 4 3   02 03 04 05 06

Printed in the U.S.A.   08
First trade printing, August 2002

Expert reader: Lisa Mielke
Assistant Director of Education
New York Aquarium
Brooklyn, NY

The dolphins on the cover are bottlenose dolphins.
Common dolphins are on the title page.
The dolphin on page 3 is an Amazon River dolphin.

For Adam and Daniel Parker, with love
—M. and G. Berger

To Jo Gauer, who just saw her first wild dolphin
—K. Carr

INTRODUCTION

Dolphins are remarkable animals. They have been part of people's lives for thousands of years. The ancient Greeks considered dolphins sacred. Sailors have long believed that dolphins near a ship signal a good voyage.

Everyone loves dolphins' grace and beauty. People flock to aquariums and zoos to see dolphins. We watch *Free Willy* and *Flipper* movies and television shows.

But people also harm dolphins. Hunters catch and kill dolphins for food, for sport, or by accident. Some dolphins die as a result of pollution or injuries from passing boats. A drop in the dolphin population is the sad outcome.

Now, though, new laws protect the dolphins. Research is helping these important sea animals survive in the wild.

Is a Dolphin a Fish? presents some of the most interesting and amazing facts about dolphins.

Did you know, for example, that dolphins—

• are among the smartest of all animals?

• can look out for danger even when asleep?

• can "see" objects in the water by making sounds and listening for the echoes?

So—dive right in and read about our friends in the sea!

Melvin Berger   *Gilda Berger*

THE WORLD OF DOLPHINS

Is a dolphin a fish?

No. A dolphin is actually a small whale. And all whales are mammals—just like you.

Mammals are born alive, feed on their mothers' milk, breathe air, and are warm-blooded. Fish hatch from eggs, find their own food from birth, get oxygen from the water, and are cold-blooded. Dolphins and fish are very different animals indeed!

Do dolphins swim like fish?

No. Dolphins move their horizontal tail fins, called flukes, up and down. Fish swing their vertical tails from side to side. Most dolphins also have two flippers for steering and a back, or dorsal, fin that keeps them from rolling over.

How fast do dolphins swim?

About 12 miles an hour (19 kph)—the speed of fast human runners. But most dolphins can swim even faster in short bursts if necessary. When chased by sharks they can zip along at more than 25 miles an hour (40 kph). When tracking prey, the biggest dolphin, the orca, can top 40 miles an hour (64 kph)!

Dolphins also hitch rides in the bow waves behind fast-moving boats or whiz along on the crests of ordinary waves. Surfers know how that works!

Do dolphins dive?

Yes. Some plunge as deep as 1,000 feet (300 m). On the way down, water pressure squeezes their bodies and makes them smaller. Now heavier than water, they dive more easily.

Atlantic humpback dolphins

Amazon River dolphins

Where do most dolphins live?

In warm or temperate oceans. There are 32 species, or kinds, of ocean dolphins. While most swim in warm seas, a few species are found in cold polar waters.

Five species of dolphins, called river dolphins, live in freshwater rivers. Compared to ocean dolphins, river dolphins have longer snouts and smaller fins. Their fins look like little lumps or ridges on their backs. Also, the eyes of river dolphins are smaller and most don't see as well as their ocean cousins. After all, sight is not much help in the dark, muddy waters they swim in!

Where do river dolphins live?

In South America and Asia. Amazon River dolphins of northern South America swim in groups of up to 20 animals. They spend most of their time at the river bottom hunting for small fish. When the dolphins come to the surface to breathe, they roll over gently. During the rainy season they swim among the trees in the flooded rain forest seeking food.

You can find large numbers of Francisciana, or La Plata, dolphins in ocean waters along the eastern coast of South America. Oddly enough, none live in the La Plata River!

The Ganges River dolphin of India and the Indus River dolphin of Pakistan are two Asian species. Nearly blind, they use their long beaks to pull fish and crabs from the muddy river bottoms. The extremely rare Chinese river dolphin, or Beiji, lives in the Yangtze River. According to an ancient Chinese legend, a beautiful princess drowned in the Yangtze and came back to Earth as a Beiji. Today, many people in China consider the Beiji a sacred animal.

Did dolphins always live in water?

No. Dolphin ancestors probably lived on land. They were four-legged animals, similar to today's cows and pigs. But over millions of years, these creatures got used to living in water. Eventually they became the animals we call dolphins.

The belief that dolphins were once land creatures comes from a study of dolphin skeletons. The two small, unattached hip bones in the rear part of the dolphin's body were where the hind limbs were attached. And some dolphins still have five short, stubby finger bones in their front flippers.

Are dolphin bones the same as yours?

No. Dolphin bones are lighter. They're sponge-like, with lots of tiny holes filled with fat and oil. Since dolphins live in water, they do not need strong bones to support their bodies. Also, light bones make it easier for these creatures to float and swim.

How big are dolphins?

They range in size. The best-known bottlenose measures up to 13 feet (4 m) long and weighs about 600 pounds (272 kg).

Common dolphins are much smaller. These animals are about 8 feet (2.4 m) long and 170 pounds (77 kg) in weight.

Bottlenose dolphin

Which are the largest dolphins?

Orcas, sometimes called killer whales. A male orca can be up to 30 feet (9 m) long and weigh as much as 10 tons (10.2 t). You can't miss these familiar dolphins—with their shiny black bodies, white undersides, and big white spots behind each eye.

Orca

Which are the smallest dolphins?

The heaviside dolphins. They are only about 4 feet (1.2 m) long and weigh about 88 pounds (40 kg).

These dolphins got their name from a certain Captain Haviside who brought the first one to England in 1827. Since then, an extra e was added to the name. Heaviside dolphins are among the smallest of all sea mammals.

Heaviside dolphin

Bottlenose dolphin

How do dolphins keep warm?

Like all mammals, dolphins change food into heat energy. This helps them maintain the same body temperature all the time. That is why we say that they're warm-blooded.

A thick layer of fat, or blubber, beneath their skin also helps dolphins stay warm. It holds in the body's heat—just like heavy clothes or a thick blanket.

A dolphin's body temperature usually stays between 96° and 98° Fahrenheit (35.5° and 36.6° C). This is slightly cooler than your normal body temperature.

How do dolphins cool off?

With built-in air-conditioning. If dolphins swim fast for a long time they can become overheated. Then the dolphins' bodies automatically send more blood to their skin and flippers. The extra heat passes into the water—and the dolphins cool off!

Do dolphins have hair or fur?

No. Dolphin skin is soft and smooth. Hairy or rough skin would make it hard to glide through the water.

Dolphins are born with a few tiny hairs or whiskers around their beaks. But they soon lose them—and are completely bald!

What color are most dolphins?

Various shades of gray. But a few kinds have extra colors or markings. The striped dolphin is dark gray or brown with a black stripe from head to tail. The spotted dolphin is basically gray with white spots on the top of its body and dark spots on the lower part. And the hourglass dolphin has an hourglass marked in black and white on its sides.

Do dolphins have noses?

Yes. A dolphin breathes through a hole on top of its head, called a blowhole. During a dive, strong muscles automatically shut the blowhole so water does not come in and drown the dolphin.

How often do dolphins breathe?

Usually once or twice a minute. Since dolphins have lungs, they must swim up to the water's surface to get a breath of air. But during a dive, some hold their breath much longer.

Compared to us, dolphins have much better lung power. When we take a deep breath, we only fill about 30 percent of our lungs with air. When a dolphin breathes, air takes up a full 80 percent of its lungs!

Do dolphins sleep?

Yes, but not like you do. Scientists think that when a dolphin sleeps, half its brain remains awake and alert. That's because dolphins don't breathe automatically, like humans do. They must decide when to come to the water's surface for a breath of air.

Also, sharks and other enemies can attack at any moment. Dolphins have to be ready to flee or fight—even when they're sleeping.

Are porpoises the same as dolphins?

No. But they are close relatives. Dolphins, porpoises, and all other whales are part of a group of marine mammals called cetaceans (si-TAY-shuhnz).

Most dolphins are more slender and streamlined than porpoises. Also, dolphins generally have more steeply sloping foreheads and longer, more pointed beaks than porpoises. If you could look inside their mouths, you'd see that dolphins' teeth are cone-shaped. Porpoise teeth look like little shovels.

Atlantic striped dolphin

DOLPHINS AT SEA

What are groups of dolphins called?

Herds, pods, shoals, or schools. Most dolphins in the open ocean swim in large groups. Groups of common dolphins, for example, can number in the thousands. Fraser's dolphins live in groups of 500 or more.

Dolphins that usually swim close to the coast form smaller groups. A bottlenose herd, for example, may contain only one dozen dolphins. Pods of orcas usually consist of 5 to 20 individuals.

Why do dolphins swim in groups?

To find food more easily. Dolphins, like other intelligent, social mammals such as wolves, lions, and chimpanzees, often hunt in groups.

Dusky dolphins, for example, swim around and around a school of fish until the fish are tightly packed together. Then the dolphins charge in and snap up the trapped prey.

Swimming in herds also helps dolphins defend themselves against enemy attacks. When threatened, dolphins can spread the warning and, if necessary, fight together to ward off danger.

Are all the dolphins in a herd alike?

No. Many herds contain dolphins of different species, sometimes including large whales. The main thing that keeps them together is a search for similar kinds of food. Some dolphins in a pod stay together for many years, just like you do with your friends and family. Others just come and go.

Dusky dolphins

Which is the best-known dolphin?

The bottlenose. Bottlenoses may be as long as 13 feet (4 m) and weigh about 600 pounds (272 kg). Most stay within 100 miles (160 km) of land. Because of its short beak, a bottlenose always looks like it's smiling. If you've ever seen a dolphin show at an aquarium or zoo, you've probably seen a bottlenose dolphin performing. In the wild, bottlenose dolphins swim alongside fishing boats, feeding on scraps thrown overboard. Sometimes they're joined by their smaller relatives, the common dolphins.

Bottlenose dolphins

How can you recognize common dolphins?

By their long, narrow snouts, bulging foreheads, and the dark bands around their eyes. Fast-swimming common dolphins can stay underwater for several minutes while hunting prey.

People on ships in the open ocean frequently see common dolphins swimming in large groups. Often, the dolphins follow ships for long distances, leaping high out of the water and turning somersaults as they go. They're hard to miss.

Common dolphins

What do dolphins eat?

Mostly fish and squid. The Pacific white-sided dolphin, for example, eats about 20 pounds (9 kg) of fish and squid a day. What an appetite!

Which is the biggest eater of all?

The orca. In addition to fish, orcas feed on seals, sea lions, penguins, sharks, sea turtles, and other dolphins and whales. One orca was found with the remains of 13 dolphins and 14 seals in its stomach.

Orcas sometimes surround animals they want to eat. Or, they knock seals off ice floes by ramming the ice. They swallow small prey whole and rip apart larger prey.

Would you believe that the orcas' favorite food is the lips and tongue of huge blue whales?

Squid

Orcas

Spinner dolphins

Why do some dolphins leap out of the water?

No one knows for sure. Dolphins may spy hop, or poke their heads and eyes above water to look around. Perhaps they are watching out for danger. Some experts believe that taking short jumps out of the water helps the dolphins travel faster.

Dolphins also breach. That is, they jump high above the water and land with a big splash. Breaching may be a way to scratch an itch or keep in touch with other dolphins.

Which dolphin is the best leaper?

The dusky dolphin. Sometimes, a dusky dolphin will jump up in the air 50 times in a row! Often, one will shoot up by itself and start a chain reaction in the herd. Before you know it, hundreds of duskies are leaping in and out of the water.

How did spinner dolphins get their name?

From their habit of spinning in the air as they leap out of the water. You can find spinner dolphins in the deeper parts of the Atlantic, Pacific, and Indian oceans.

Do dolphins drink salt water?

No. It would make them sick, just as you would get sick if you drank lots of seawater. Dolphins get all the water they need from the food they eat.

Do dolphins chew their food?

No. Dolphins swallow their food without chewing. All dolphin teeth are the same size and shape. Lined up in long rows, the teeth are small, sharp, and shaped like tiny ice cream cones. One look, and scientists know they're for catching food, not for chewing.

How many teeth do dolphins have?

From 100 to 200 upper and lower teeth. Only the Risso's dolphin has teeth in its lower jaw alone.

Dolphins don't lose baby teeth or grow new teeth to replace any that are knocked out or worn out. A lost tooth is lost forever.

Are dolphins always eating?

No, not always. But dolphins do eat every day—or try to. They can't go very long without food. When there is little food they live off the fat in their bodies. When there is plenty to eat, they gobble up much more than they need. This builds up their reserves of fat. No dolphin ever gets chubby from overeating. Swimming is slimming!

Do dolphins taste what they eat?

Yes. Dolphins can tell if food is sweet, sour, bitter, or salty. The dolphins in an aquarium can also tell if a fish is fresh or not. Feed a dolphin a rotten fish, and it will spit it out!

Risso's dolphin

Atlantic spotted dolphin

Do dolphins have ears?

Yes. On the outside, the ears are two tiny, hard-to-find holes in the dolphins' skin. But hidden inside their bodies are the inner ears.

By using their ears, dolphins can hear all the sounds that we can hear, as well as sounds that are beyond our range of hearing.

How do dolphins find food?

By sending out clicking sounds that reflect off fish in the water. Dolphins listen to the echoes, just as you listen to echoes in a cave. The difference is that the dolphins' echoes tell them where to find their dinner!

Echoes that return quickly tell dolphins that the prey is close. Echoes that take longer mean it is farther away. The bounced-back sounds also tell the size, speed, and direction of movement of the prey in the water.

Dolphins also use echoes to locate all sorts of other things in the water, such as boats, sharks, and other dolphins. Using echoes to spot objects is called echolocation (ek-oh-loh-KAY-shuhn).

How well do dolphins hear?

Very well. Dolphins can hear echoes over a distance of about 2,500 feet (760 m). That's about 10 times farther than they can see in water.

In experiments, dolphins using echolocation could tell the difference between balls that were 2¼ and 2½ inches (5.7 and 6.4 cm) in diameter from a distance of 5 feet (1.5 m). They could tell the difference between an object made of glass and the same object made of plastic. And they were able to avoid a wire hanging in the water that was only four-hundredths of an inch (1 mm) thick!

How do dolphins make sounds?

By forcing air out through the passage leading to their blowhole. The sound vibrations go to the big, round, fatty bulge on their foreheads, which is called a melon. The melon focuses and beams out all the different sounds that dolphins make.

How many sounds do dolphins make?

More than 30 different sounds—including brays, clicks, barks, squeals, and squawks. For example, one researcher found that a dolphin brays like a donkey when it finds food. He calls this a feeding call. As soon as the call goes out, other dolphins rush in to enjoy the feast!

How else do dolphins communicate?

They whistle. Each dolphin seems to have its own whistle almost from birth. It makes this sound when it meets another dolphin. Dolphins can also copy each other's whistles—no one is sure exactly why.

Dolphins whistle to keep track of one another in dark waters and across long distances. But only the dolphins know what they're saying to each other!

Do dolphins use body language?

Indeed they do. And experts think they know the meanings of some of the dolphins' movements. If one dolphin faces another with mouth open and back arched it means "Don't bother me!" Turning sideways with mouth closed shows surrender or giving up. Dolphins that get picked on by the rest of the herd usually swim beneath the others.

Scientists have seen mother dolphins spanking their young with their flippers. Another behavior is lobtailing, which is slapping the tail on the water's surface. This seems to tell the others, "Stay away!"

Commerson's dolphins

Can dolphins see well?

It varies. Some dolphins can see very well in water as well as in air, and in bright or dim light. Other dolphins have poorer sight. And some kinds are nearly blind.

    Dolphins have upper and lower eyelids that close when they are asleep. The lids protect the animals' eyes from enemies or dangerous objects in the water. But don't expect eyelashes or eyebrows. Dolphins don't have any!

Pantropical spotted dolphins

Can dolphins smell?

No. As far as the experts know, dolphins have no sense of smell. Why should they? Dolphins are holding their breath almost all the time!

Do dolphins have a good sense of touch?

Yes. Dolphin skin seems very sensitive to the slightest change in pressure. You often see dolphins swimming together and touching and rubbing one another as a way of keeping in contact.

Are dolphins smart?

Yes. Many scientists consider dolphins as smart as chimpanzees and dogs—the most intelligent animals of all. Dolphins have large brains, which is one sign of intelligence. In zoos and aquariums, they learn all sorts of tricks—playing catch, throwing Frisbees, leaping high to ring a bell or grab a fish, shooting baskets, and much more.

Dolphins are also curious and playful—other signs of intelligence. In the wild, dolphins often toss fish up in the air and catch them. We guess their mothers never taught them not to play with their food!

How do trainers teach dolphins "tricks"?

They reward them when they do the trick correctly. The reward is usually a fish.

Listen and watch carefully at the next aquarium show you go to. The dolphins will—

- go to a spot at the poolside.
- watch the trainer's hand signals and do their tricks.
- hear a whistle that tells them they are done.
- return to the poolside to get their reward.

Can humans "talk" to dolphins?

Yes. People use whistle signals for different commands. Underwater speakers send the whistles through the dolphin pool to the animals. In this way, scientists teach dolphins simple sentences.

The first sentence a scientist taught Nat, a young male dolphin, was "towel/over." When Nat heard the whistles for this command, he jumped over a towel floating on the water. He also learned "rock/retrieve," which told him to pick up a rock on the bottom of the pool. Nat learned 27 different two-word sentences by the time the study ended.

A year later a TV crew came to visit. The scientists played the whistles for Nat. To their amazement, the dolphin still remembered 25 of the 27 commands!

Bottlenose dolphins

Bottlenose dolphin

Do dolphins travel far?

Some do. Many dolphins travel hundreds of miles (kilometers) to find food. Some, including spotted dolphins and northern right whale dolphins, swim from deep ocean water to coastal water, following large schools of fish. Others, like bottlenose dolphins, usually stay close to land. But when food is scarce, they travel to the open ocean to find new sources of food.

Bottlenoses may also migrate because of water temperature. They swim toward warmer water in cold weather and back to cooler water in the spring.

What is a dolphin stranding?

Animals stuck on a beach when the tide goes out. Often the stranded dolphins are sick or dying.

Sometimes numbers of healthy dolphins end up stranded on a beach for unknown reasons. If these dolphins are not helped back into the water, they will die.

How long do dolphins live?

To at least 25 years of age. The longest life span of a dolphin on record is 32 years.

How do scientists study dolphins?

In various ways. To learn about dolphin communication, scientists record and analyze the sounds dolphins make underwater. With powerful sonar, special airplanes, and research ships they spot and track dolphin herds. Sometimes they even mount a small radio transmitter on a dolphin's fin to follow its movements.

Veterinarians treat sick and injured dolphins. They use medical tests, X rays, and medicine to help dolphins stay healthy.

THE LIFE OF DOLPHINS

When do dolphins mate?

Mostly in spring or early summer. Male dolphins are called bulls; females are called cows. Cows are pregnant for between 9 and 14 months before they give birth to calves.

Where are dolphin calves born?

Right in the water. Calves are born tail first.

Immediately after birth, the cow lunges away from the calf. This breaks the long, ropelike tube, called the umbilical cord, that connected the calf to its mother.

Quickly the cow, and sometimes other female adults called "aunts," help the newborn calf swim up to the surface. Here the calf takes its first breath of air.

How many calves are born at one time?

Usually one. Occasionally a cow may give birth to twin calves—but as a rule only one survives.

Do dolphin calves look like the adults?

Yes, except that they are much smaller. In fact, baby dolphins are only about one-third the size of their parents.

In some species, the calf's colors or markings are also different from those of its parents. For example, spotted dolphin calves are born without spots. The spots only appear as the calves get older.

Hector's dolphin and calf

Are dolphins good parents?

Yes, excellent ones. Like all female mammals, the mother has special glands that produce milk. She squeezes rich, heavy milk from her nipples into the calf's mouth. The mother does this every 15 minutes or so, all day long for a year or more.

Some adult males swim among the females and their calves, even though the males don't help to care for the young. Females from the herd protect the calf while the mother feeds.

When do calves eat their first fish?

At about six months of age. They swallow small fish whole. But if a calf catches a large fish it sometimes rubs it on the ocean floor or smacks it on the surface of the water to break it into bite-size pieces. And even after it begins to catch its own fish, the dolphin calf continues to nurse.

Finless dolphins and calves

Do baby dolphins cry?

No. Baby dolphins only look like they're crying. A special liquid covers their eyes, keeping them moist and well protected in the salt water. The liquid makes the babies' eyes look like they are full of tears—but they are not.

When are dolphins old enough to have babies?

Different species are ready at different ages. For example, striped dolphins can bear young when they are six to nine years old. Bottlenose dolphins take a little longer. They don't usually mature until they're between eight and ten years of age.

Are dolphins social animals?

Yes. They seem to enjoy being with other dolphins, swimming, leaping, and chasing fish together. Cows and calves stay very close for up to six years—or longer.

Quite often two male dolphins pair up for life. They swim side by side, and even come up for air together. Experts think the pairing helps them fight off their enemies.

If a dolphin is sick or injured, other dolphins care for it. They nudge it along with their flippers and bodies so it can stay with the group. And they push it up to the surface to breathe.

Do dolphins rescue people?

Yes. The earliest story about dolphins saving people dates back to ancient Greece over 2,000 years ago. The musician Arion was returning home by boat after winning a prize for singing. Some evil sailors wanted to kill him and steal his treasure.

Arion asked to sing one last song. As he did, dolphins started to swim alongside the boat. Seeing them, Arion jumped into the water. One dolphin carried him to safety on its back. Since ancient times, people have believed that dolphins bring good luck.

Have there been any modern-day dolphin rescues?

Yes. One happened in 1983. A helicopter crashed in the Java Sea. The pilot managed to get out and climb into a rubber life raft. Soon a dolphin swam alongside and began pushing the raft through the water. For nine days the dolphin nudged the raft forward. At long last, it shoved the raft up on a sandy beach.

Do dolphins save people out of kindness?

Probably not. Scientists say it's part of the dolphin's nature to help other dolphins that are in trouble. And most likely it is that instinct that leads them to save people.

Bottlenose dolphin

Can dolphins stop shark attacks?

Sometimes. Dolphins generally flee approaching sharks. But if this fails, they stay and fight. The dolphins often drive the sharks away by ramming them with their beaks.

Sharks are definitely the dolphins' worst enemies. About one out of every four dolphins has scars or cuts from battles with sharks.

Tiger shark

Tucuxi

How do dolphins help fishermen?

By driving fish into fishermen's nets. Fishermen on Africa's west coast set their nets close to shore. Then they slap big, broad sticks on the water. The noise attracts Atlantic humpback dolphins and bottlenose dolphins. As they swim toward the sound, the dolphins drive whole schools of fish before them—and into the nets.

Which fish often swim with dolphins?

Tuna fish. Tuna fish and dolphins are often found together since they both eat the same prey. The tuna usually swim underneath the dolphins. When sharks approach from below, the tuna scatter. This warns the dolphins to speed away. In turn, dolphins help the tuna find food, since they're better at it. That's natural cooperation!

Do dolphins ever attack other dolphins?

Yes. Male dolphins sometimes fight one another to win mates or to protect their feeding rights. Scientists have seen dolphins slap each other with their flukes, whack others with their jaws, and bite their enemies. At times adult dolphins even eat young or smaller dolphins!

Do dolphins kill people?

No. Until now, dolphins have never killed, or even seriously hurt, anyone.

Yet as tourists come in closer contact with wild dolphins the danger grows. In recent years, several people have been bitten, battered, or pulled underwater by dolphins in special resorts where there are "swim with the dolphins" activities. Many experts fear that too much contact between humans and dolphins may lead to more accidents—or even deaths. We must never forget that dolphins are wild creatures and should be approached very carefully.

Do people kill dolphins?

Yes. Some fishermen kill dolphins by accident. Since dolphins and tuna fish often swim in the same waters, the fishermen set their nets where they see leaping dolphins. Dolphins get caught and tangled in nets intended for the tuna. The dolphins are unable to escape and get to the surface to breathe. Thousands of dolphins die this way.

Other dolphins are killed on purpose. Some are caught for sport. Also, certain fishermen believe that dolphins prey on the fish they're trying to catch. So they kill the dolphins for stealing their fish—even though dolphins catch many fewer fish than people do!

What is "Dolphin Safe"?

A program to save dolphins. "Dolphin Safe" encourages fishermen to use nets with a very fine mesh. This helps prevent dolphins from getting tangled in the nets.

"Dolphin Safe" also works in another way. Divers go into the nets to free any dolphins that are trapped. Then workers haul in the nets with only tuna.

Does pollution kill dolphins?

Yes. Humans harm dolphins by polluting the water. The runoff from farms and street waste in city sewers are very dangerous sources of pollution. Also harmful are chemical wastes from factories or homes, which people dump either in oceans or in rivers that flow into oceans. Dolphins also die from eating plastic trash that they mistake for something good to eat.

Do people eat dolphins?

Some do. In Japan and a few other countries, ocean dolphins are a great delicacy. But the dolphin that appears on some menus in North America is not a true dolphin. It is a fish, which is also known as mahimahi or dorado.

Atlantic spotted dolphins

INDEX

About the Authors

Like most people, the Bergers love reading, hearing about, and visiting dolphins. They have worked with many organizations and individuals to help stop dolphins from drowning in fishing nets intended to catch tuna.

About the Illustrator

While working on this book, Karen Carr went snorkeling in the Caribbean with her daughter and husband. On their trip, they met a dolphin named Jo Jo. "Jo Jo lives alone in the wild, but likes to visit people," Karen said. "My daughter is called Jo Jo, too! It was a wonderful experience."